Eyes With Pride

Mandi Dellagicoma

Presentation by *BookLeaf Publishing*

Web: www.bookleafpub.com

E-mail: info@bookleafpub.com

ISBN: 9789358318241

First edition 2024

DEDICATION

To everyone in the band and theater programs
at WMHS, past and present,

Thank you for becoming my family and making
all the hours worth it.

ACKNOWLEDGEMENT

If it weren't for taking Creative Writing my senior year, I never would have written poetry. I was downright dreading it when I saw it on the syllabus but as it turned out, it was my favorite unit and I fell in love with it. And that is only due to the incredible guidance of Laura DeSena, my teacher for both creative writing classes. I never would have tried poetry if it wasn't for her classes. She knew just how to guide us and make writing poetry not only enjoyable but a remarkable form of self expression. She also created a space where we could share our work and both receive and share constructive feedback with one another. I'm so grateful to have had that opportunity.

Additionally, out of everything I've written, the thing that has inspired me the most has been my time in the West Milford High School Theater program. It was one of the best things I've ever been a part of and that is mostly due to Heather Burns, my theater teacher who has done so much for me and for the program all together. She not only makes incredible theater students but an incredible atmosphere where we can work together to create a show and strong connections with each other that last.

PREFACE

I'm so excited to have the opportunity to do this. The following poems are my way of showing my love for what they're about. The programs I was able to be a part of, the friends I made, the wild range of emotions that came with things like graduation, and even just the beautiful nature of my hometown were all things that have left a lasting impact on me and all things I'm so grateful for. This is my way of preserving them and showing my love for them.

It's Like Home

It has a familiar feeling even though it's a world
I've never been to
It's a world that has never nor will ever exist
But it exists to me
To others who has seeked asylum within it's
pages
You find something that connects with you and
that's all it takes
It's truly remarkable
You follow the narrative created for you by the
artists of words
But then you create the world
You create every inch of the world and watch the
story unfold
And it allows for peace, for escape, for the
chance to play the heroes
It's a playground for the mind's eye
And within those that are the best, sewn are
seeds of reality and truth
Messages that ring true from our world to theirs
Ones that we so desperately wish to see
And that makes our imaginary worlds all the
more powerful
Because not only do we get to live in bold and
exciting worlds

But we get to live in worlds where our strongest
morals can fight and win the day
But eventually we walk the final steps in the
narrative and retire it to the shelf
It collects dust as it sits in moments ever frozen
There it remains
Until you return to it
And it's all still there, preserved perfectly how
you left it
You forgot the complete and total impact it had
on you
It welcomes you back with open arms and you
can't help but delve into it
You return home

Music Is

Chilling
Magic
Calm
Serenity
Familiarity
Pain
A call to action
A weapon of mass destruction
Beauty incarnate
A power known to only so many
A symbol of solidarity
A symbol of hope
A tool of poets
The language of lovers
Creation and Destruction
Open arms
An extended hand
A venomous bite
A loving touch
A challenge
An art
Notes on a staff
Ink on a page
Concepts waiting to be played
That's all music is

Breathe

Deep breath
In… out…
Locked in
Competition time
Rehearsal went well, warm-ups were good
Now it's focus
The field is still
Time is nonexistent
There is a united feel on the field
It's that feeling where anxiety has been beating
you into the ground all day and finally, finally it
lets up
It lets you breathe
It lets you feel the excited flutters in your stomach
And it lets you lock in and focus
You don't think about it
You don't notice time has passed
You go to a different place, getting in the zone
Nothing outside the show exists and you leave it
all out on the field
Then when it's over, you get the rush of joy and
relief
You can appreciate what you've done
And you just countdown the days until the next
show

In the Dark of the Bus

Two shimmering smiles
A first place win taken home
In the dark of the bus
Sweeping exhaustion
An hour long bus ride ahead
In the dark of the bus
Bright laughter, warm smiles
Filling up and lighting up
The dark of the bus
Surrounded by friends
So many good memories
In the dark of the bus
Until one day you
Realize it's all gone
In the dark of the bus

Dayton Trip: The Loss

That's it
It's over
Not the trip, but the show
Never to be performed or lived again
And we didn't even know it was the last
After that realization, the realization of defeat
Mood deflate
Everyone holds back emotions to spare
themselves and others
It's solemn and somber, and near silent
They didn't even need to announce our defeat
The knowledge of it burns a hole into your heart
A hole bored by pain and guilt and anger
Why weren't we good enough? Why wasn't I
good enough? Why weren't they good enough?
But there comes a time when those questions
grow tiresome

When all the cliche messages of optimism start
to shine a weak light
Maybe that is all that matters,
That we thought we did good
Maybe there was a reason we didn't make it
further
Now we can relax and make memories with one
another
Maybe all this pain that only gets irritated with
being constantly surrounded by what beat us is
our hurdle to pass
To pass onto a happier place
Is it as happy as we would have been?
No, but it's still happy
It's still a memory I wouldn't trade for the world

Dayton Trip: The Final Hours

The morning was a sleepy flurry
Loading everyone and everything
Then slowly one by one everyone fell to slumber
The journey was long and once everyone awoke,
the mood was light
The trip had had its ups and it's downs
It's wins and one very brutal loss
But this ride was the conclusion of our journey
Both the physical trip and also our season, our
show, and for all of the seniors, our time with
the group
Forever
So we spent the time in joy
Laughter and stories filled the air as nature's
beauty passed by in a constant stream
The air was giddy with joy that no annoyances
could stifle
Despite the long ride, no one minded because we
were happy, happy from the moment and the
memories from the season and the trip
The games we played, the spectacles we saw, the
smiles we shared

Hours upon hours later, we were at the end
There would be no more bus rides, no more
practices, no more competitions
Nothing
We would arrive at the school, back up our
equipment, and then go our separate ways
Our show would never exist again, nor our
group, our family we created
It would be over but it will live on in the
invaluable memories we made
As we pull down the familiar roads to the end, I
couldn't help but smile

The Break of Day

Sunlight breaks its path over the earth
It's soft touch stretching over the land
Light and fleeting, a whisper of a moment
It takes time to build into the day
It wakes slowly, jumping from each plant and
creature
Slowly waking the world
It warms the leaves on the trees and the creeping
river
The waters growing colder by each day.
The crystalline night slowly cracking away for
the sun
It is a new day
The pains of yesterday may die with yesterday
Things will move forward as time does
Leaving everything beyond and lighting up
something new
The world has waken and begins to turn
The red yellow and green leaves open to greet
the sun
A soft chilled breeze fills the air as well
Regardless of the day before, the morning has
arrived

Storm Sky

I love a storm sky
It's somehow both bright and dark at the same
time
Gray clouds come rolling in and hang low in the
sky
The winds whip up and rustles the trees
The trees, they know when a storm is coming
They bend and sway with the breeze
And they do something else
My grandfather taught me about it;
The leaves will turn upside down when rain is
coming to collect the water better
I don't know if it's true
But I like to believe it is

Through the Trees

Next to the rushing river bringing life to the
world
Stood towers of nature with light shimmering
through
It's something out of a fairy tale that exists
within our world
No matter where you are it's the same, beautiful
air
With the same beautiful light flickering past the
leaves
Above you is a kaleidoscope of nature's beauty
Reds and greens and oranges and yellows
painted on the leaves, splashes of the blue sky
peaking out
The light dances through the blue and down to
the earth
Down to the soft moss that carpets the forest
floor

The forest floor that gives way to life and is
freckled with sun spots
The trees sway and dance with the wind
Leaves swirl and twirl down to the earth to settle
to sleep
A chill in on the wind but it doesn't quell the
mood
The spirit in the air is unparalleled
Beauty and calm and life
Pure life is what fills the air and inspires
happiness and peace

Anything Goes and Everything Stops

There's a moment
A life stilling moment most can remember
I can remember exactly where I was
The halting feeling and the unknown
So sure of the future one moment and so scared
the next
Sitting in the seats of the auditorium, I can
remember all being called there
We knew something was on the horizon
There were rumors and meetings but we tried to
ignore it
Not because we didn't want to know but because
we didn't want to believe
Then we were told.
It would just be two weeks
Two weeks and we would be able to return to
our show on our stage
Just two weeks

We continued with what we could
For the first time, "virtual" joined our
vocabulary in the spotlight
Virtual school
Virtual rehearsal
We tried to say it was fine
That it was nice just being able to be together
and it was funny sometimes
But then two weeks turned into four which
turned into six which turned into indefinite
We gave up
The shell of what we loved sat alone
Baren and blocked away
We didn't know it would be last time dazzling
lights would grace that set
But there came a point where we knew
There would be no more dazzling lights upon it
ever again

Base Coat

Base coat. Noun. A first coat of a surfacing
material, as paint.
Underlying the finish coat and consisting of a
single coat
Ours is this grayish, brownish, taupe color
It's step two
Step one is build the sets and get everything up
Step two is cover everything in a base coat
This is one of the longest steps
Suddenly one day, there's a little splotch of base
coat paint then each day it spreads and spreads
and
Spreads across the whole set
It gets everywhere: on you, on the walls, on the
stage
Everything around you is suddenly this shade of
grayish, brownish, taupe
But there's more too it, it's not just to prime the
set
It's to cover up the old ones
We reuse the same walls and wood; show after
show, year after year.
That means as we build the sets, we piece
together old shows in a nostalgic patchwork

Adams family walls on the anything goes deck
with the anastasia posts and the 12 angry jurors
door
It's sentimental, looking at all the old paint and
reliving memories from those shows
But then there comes a point it has to get painted
It hurts a bit, remembering the countless hours
you spent painting everything but
It's the cycle of the show
Those sets had layers and layers of paint
underneath what you remember
Layers of memories and shows
But that's the beauty of it
You get to turn all these crystals of memory into
the chandelier of a set
Then you take the same taupe color that those
memories are built on and you cover everything,
a phoenix being reborn into new life
Now the next year, you will look upon the
Adams family walls on the anything goes deck
with the anastasia posts and the 12 angry jurors
door
Simply as pieces of the Something Rotten set
And that's the purpose of base coat- to create the
canvas for memories to be built

A Show

It starts as nothing
Merely an idea, a title
Yes, there are other versions out there
somewhere
But it's not ours
No yet

It's starts slowly at first
A long process then slower and slower still
Then we think will pick up and it snails by
But slowly it gains life
Just flickers of it
And family begins to grow
Despite some fighting and short tempers,
It's a warm feeling of eternity, purgatory

Then one day it picks up speed
Suddenly there are days left, not months
The rush stars to come in
It's too much to do in too little time
Everyone's in a sprint to the finish line

And we get there and stop
We realize that it's over
It suddenly has an expiration date
It's slipping away
In days, not months, it will be gone
And then we are left with memories
Merely a memory

And it is ours

It was ours

My Home

It's over and it was spectacular
Every moment was precious and partly because
there's an end
There was a deadline and we reached it
It's now a lovely dream
But from every dream you must awake to reality
Reality that is filled with tension and pain and
frustration
Reality where it is not as beautiful as a dream
Where you are not as valued
Where it is not a family of unconditional respect
and love
But one of tension and walking upon glass
And if that is the case then is it truly your family
Or is your family that kaleidoscope of people
A collection of people who all run from reality
and find each other

Find each other in a world they all have a hand
to create
To create an intricate story and world
A world where both on and off stage they love
each other
Love each other in almost every sense of the
word
Love each other unconditionally
Unconditionally respect and care for each other
Care about things because you care about them
Care about you even when your family doesn't
Because then that isn't your family and that isn't
your home
They are your family and this is your home

Empty Theater

It's a rare occurrence
I've seen it a handful of times
It's when this place of home and love and life is
void of the latter but grows stronger in the
formers
It makes no sense
But it sits there silently as you enter
It's like a comforting friend
It doesn't speak but it lends an ear
It provides solace from the outside world
Which is something invaluable
It allows for quiet reflection amidst your refuge
Reflection on your friendships and joys in that
room
On the healing from pains outside that room
All the laughter, the tears, the giddiness, the
sorrow in that room
Time is short but there
There is eternal,
Your eternal sanctuary

"Rising Curtains Draped Upon Hallowed Halls"

Rising curtains draped upon hallowed halls
Beautiful rivers of velvet and rope
A thousand lives lived within these four walls
Lives of emotion; of love, loss, fear and hope

Hours upon hours upon this wood
Forging a new life faster than the day
Giving oneself over to the world if one would
Be then immersed in whatever may

But as lights arise, the lives emerge there
To be lived once and then once again and again
To live only with love, without despair
Lights and life stave off the lingering pain

Oh to live a thousand lives all at once
As beautiful and as rare an occurrence.

September 3rd, 2021

I wasn't very close to you.
I knew you a bit
You were one of the nicest people I've met
You showed me that theater was a home
That people there were amazing and kind and
were a family
And even after you graduated, you were still
there, still making people smile
I remember one of the first days I met you
It was during my class and you were goofing
around with the other tech kids
Proving how close they all were and what
someone could get from this program
You made me want to join tech, where I found
my future
I remember the day you came back the next
year, grinning and making people smile
It was a stressful day and you brought light and
calm to it
And I remember the day you died
I remember waking up in the morning and
seeing the messages from my theater group chat
The pain and shock palpable even through text
messages

Two days later we were in school, the first day
back
There was a heavy grief in the room even if no
one mentioned it until the end
Your shadow lingered the whole year
I remember the day during the musical when
Burns came up to me
She asked me to add a picture of you to the
projection cues
When she went on stage after bows
She never does that
Then she named the booth after you
I remember feeling silent tears fall down as I
watched the cast,
All shocked and on the verge of tears I
remember the curtains closing and rushing back
there
Everyone crying and hugging each other
I went up to Tori and she hugged me tighter than
anyone
She was sobbing, crying out about how unfair it
is that you're gone
Everyone was crying and holding onto each
other like castaways in a storm
I had never seen some of them cry before
The pain and love and loss in that room was
overwhelming
I remember attending a football game,
September 2nd, 2022

Someone got hurt, seriously hurt
It felt like hours as he laid there and coaches
hurried to help
And then the ambulance pulled onto the field to
help him
I remember freezing and my heart racing and
tears threatening to fall
Because I remember driving home on September
3rd, 2021
When my mom was late because of some
accident and we had to go around it
But we still came out right across from the cops
and ambulances
I only saw pieces of the crash but what I
followed was the ambulance in front of us
The ambulance that was speeding ahead of us
and taking the turn away down the road
I couldn't go to the funeral, I wasn't very close
to you and I couldn't see them all crying
But every day I drive past your memorial where
the crash happened
I remember all of it every day
And every day I flash my headlights three times
when I pass
Saying hi, good bye, and thank you
Remembering you
In that way, I'm now very close to you

Us

We didn't set out to find each other
We didn't know we'd find each other
We all started this at different times
All coming in alone in some way or another
But over 4 years as some left and some joined
We stayed
In some way or another we stayed
We went through joys and pains
We went through the dark and the light
And we didn't realize we were together
Not until it's time for us to leave
We're at peace and help one another
We work to build each up, even if it's hard
We've bonded over the most obscure things
Things we never considered
Giant clubs, communists, hung juries, eggs, krill
Things that make us smile at the mere mention
Things we don't realize made an impact
Unit it's over
Like us
We didn't know what we have until it's about to
end
We didn't set out to find each other
But I'm glad we did

How

You have no idea how much you mean to me;
How much you affect my life
How often to make me smile just by walking in
the room
How every story you tell me brightens my day
How the way you joke around with me makes
me so happy
How our growing relationships means the world
to me
How your support carries me through my fears
How your concern heals my worries
How bonding over stupid shows makes them all
the better
How the way you defend me reassures me
How commiserating relieves some misery
How talking about the day makes it so much
better
How dreaming about the future makes it feel
real
How even little conversations turn my day
around
How I physically cannot be sad around you guys
How you're all my family
And all while you have no idea how.

In the Blink of an Eye

You know when you're driving and you pass an
interesting car on the road?
Maybe an interesting license plate or bumper
sticker or something on the car
But whatever it was it's gone in a moment
In the blink of an eye, they're gone
You might remember them for a while but
eventually they're gone there too
If you're lucky you might drive with beside
them for a while
Miles even
You expect them next to you and you hope they
find you just as interesting
You both go through a lot in miles, even in just 4
miles
But then it's time to take different exits
And then they're gone
Gone in a moment
4 miles to know each other and
In the blink of an eye
They're gone

The Curved Corner

I was leaving one day and found myself
stopping
Stopped on the sidewalk where it curve a corner,
coming out of the auditorium facing the middle
school
I was overtaken
By the once blistering air settling into a cool
mild breeze
The immense feeling of security it brought
The flowering trees by the flag pole swaying in
it
Petals fluttering around as they settled on the
earth
The light that was kind as it dipped behind the
hills and trees
The silence
The serenity
The beauty
The reassurance
I remembered all the memories here, memories I
have from that corner

I remember the hundreds of times I've walked
around it with friends from band
I remember the hundreds of times I've walked
around it alone from band
I remember arriving to rehearsals on saturdays
for band and theater
I remember laughing and bonding with my
friends as we're locked out and waiting
I remember all the late late nights leaving and
walking that way to my car where I didn't leave
for another hour, caught up talking
I remember the day in 2021 as we got close to
the musical and it was still the midst of covid so
we rolled out the stashed lunch tables out onto
that corner and sidewalk and we had lunch out
there on the day of our long tech rehearsal
I remember the joy that day brought
There are seldom few memories left to make
there
But by god, I'll cherish the ones I have for the
rest of my life.

The Way It Is

When a group becomes a family
It is inherently doomed
This is simply the way it is
When a program has members of all ages It will
inevitably lead to heart break This is simply the
way it is
When each flute and each actor is a different
grade And each year another drum has to say
goodbye Something rare is created
Something beautiful and impactful
Something that is not permanent
Each year a new family is created
A new show and a new life
A year is spent bonding and building
Growing and grieving
Until it stops
A part of the family moves one

The moment in time of which the show existed
is gone It goes from smiling to smiled
It will never exist again
That is simply the passage of time
And yet that is the beauty of it
It is special and sacred
As fleeting as the notes of a violin
And it is loved because it happed far more than
it is mourned because it's lost
When a moment becomes a memory
It is eternally cherished
This is simply the way it is

www.ingramcontent.com/pod-product-compliance
Lightning Source LLC
Chambersburg PA
CBHW071236140726
47996CB00007B/2624